Crossing by Ferry

Crossing by Ferry

Poems New and Selected

Donald Junkins

The University of Massachusetts Press
Amherst, 1978

The author wishes to acknowledge his gratitude to the National Endowment for the
Arts for a Creative Writing Fellowship Grant which helped make this book possible.

"Walden in July" (p. 51), copyright © 1962 by The New Yorker Magazine, Inc.;
"Approaches to Blue Hill Bay: Chart No. 13313 (p. 3), copyright © 1977 by The
New Yorker Magazine, Inc.; "Walden in January" is reprinted with permission of
Choice: A Magazine of Poetry and Graphics; "On the Lawn of the Mental Hospital
with Susan, My Student" first appeared in *Paintbrush* 2 (Autumn 1974); "Hitting
Fungos in Austin, Texas" is reprinted by permission from *Willmore City*; "Drewry's
Bluff, Virginia, May 16, 1864," "Robert Junkins, Captured at Dunbar, Scotland
1650: Died York, Maine 1699," "Autumn in Georgia," "The Inheritance," "Ante-
lopes," and "For Robert Kennedy: Sunderland, June 8, 1968" are reprinted from
The Massachusetts Review, copyright © 1967, 1968 by The Massachusetts Review,
Inc.; "Look—it's a purple finch!" and "Westward of Swan's Island" are reprinted
by permission from *The Poetry Miscellany*; "Uncle Harry: Shooting Partridge, 1941,"
copyright © 1971 by The Atlantic Monthly Company, Boston, Massachusetts.
Reprinted with permission; "Ten years from now you'll walk these woods alone,"
copyright © 1973 by The Antioch Review, Inc. First published in *The Antioch
Review*, Volume 32, number 3. Reprinted by the permission of the editors. Other
poems appeared previously in *Poetry, The Minnesota Review, Sumac, Hearse, The
Northwest Review, Arion's Dolphin, The Virginia Quarterly Review, Poetry Now*,
and *Poetry Miscellany*. Earlier versions of additional poems appeared in *The Sewanee
Review, The Massachusetts Review, Yankee, The Boston Review*, and *The Berkshire
Anthology*. Also, present or earlier versions appeared in *The Sunfish and the Par-
tridge* (1965), *The Graves of Scotland Parish* (1969), *And Sandpipers She Said* (copy-
right © 1970 by The University of Massachusetts Press), and *The Uncle Harry Poems
and Other Maine Reminiscences* (1977), by Donald Junkins. "Fay Winfield" first
published in *The Beloit Poetry Journal*.

Mardie

that first time, we fell asleep
next to the barred window, the cellar
of the president's house, roses I picked
the hips off outside, cars, Storrow
Drive, the house a giant head circling
over our heads (I kept breaking
bottles, filling the holes with glass,
river rats coming, new holes
beside the roses every day—the president's
wife at breakfast on the upstairs patio:
"The roses—just stunning!") Walking St. Mary's
Street that evening, the fifties, a seminary
at our backs, the soft spring rain wove
bullseye branch designs at every streetlamp grove.

Contents

4   TO THE COAST

5   CROSSING BY FERRY

1   Processions

"Approaches to Blue Hill Bay": Chart No. 13313

Late June, walking the deer runs
to Goose Pond after supper
summer begins. Sidestepping
stormblown poplars,
dry-wading the slash from the pulpers' camps
ten years ago, keeping the imaginary
straight line from Duck Island Light to the north side
of Goose Pond Mountain in our minds' eyes; poking
our fish poles through young hackmatack
straight-arms, trying to keep from snagging
the green fur, the purple stars in the schooldesk landscape
of the nautical chart.
     Yellow, blue.
The island woods are yellow. The evening sun
sprays through from the other side of the evergreens.
Woodcolors, our first grade pegs
arranging. We push for the first view
of the marsh-edged shore, spruce stumpsticks
edging deep water trout
neverminding the cold. We know where we are:
a mile straight in on the yellow.
We lose our way. My son climbs a blue spruce
to see where we've been: the two Sisters,
Long Island Plantation. On the left, the Baptist
church in Atlantic. We head into the sun.

Late June, walking the deer runs
to Goose Pond after supper
summer begins suddenly. We can hear
the creeing of gulls. Beyond the trees
they are landing, taking off, landing.
Saltwhite. Freshblue. It is all
prearranged. In a minute now
we will see the pond. Nothing has changed.

The Sunfish

Slim without diet, he moves toward worms like an early bird.
Soft nibbler, heckler of fishermen, this busyfish hits
and runs. He cleans the steel hook like a dimwit.

Children love him under boats among the yellow weeds
and under the green shade of wharves for his backbone;
they dangle bait on lines that will not sound his greed.

It is all done by touch. From overhead they cannot
see his soft mail shading into black and blue,
his blood-daubed cheek, his belly orange as spawn, the hue

of silver fading toward his tail. This pip, this pun
is the harlequin of the pond. Out of the water
he fades like leather. All anglers fish for the sun.

Three Rooms and a Dream from the Thirties

Seven poplars down, the road
in front of Hjalmar Ahl's house, the path
to the high boulder for king of the rock
or flying a kite: it is six-thirty on a Saturday morning
in September, and I am seven. Up here
I can see the Atlantic on the horizon like a blue knife.
My kite is a red badge with a tail of fleece—
it glides and rattles in the wind like the Salvation Army;
my string smells of tar and brine; it is my father's
deep sea dropline—my face is all sky
and all air.
      Fly kite, fly while you can,
      our house is still asleep.
      Fly across Sunday while the leaves
      burn. Flee the hurricane
      and the bees in the cherry tree
      and Joanne the skinny. Fly kite,
      fly through the wet beard,
      come to my hand.

The wood frogs crouch near the farmer's grange
at the south end of Bauneg Beg Pond,
and I am four under the August sun,
warm on the dry and morning yellow grass,
close by the water
and the shadows of the pines,
and the sun soft on my legs and arms
as I squat and reach in the grass.

> Don't go from my hand,
> wood frog. Don't go high
> into the dry and sunburned
> grass. Stay for my hand,
> and my father's hand, and the pickerel
> that waits among the yellow weeds.

Remember the black-eyed Susans
and the crickets' high sizzle, and the morning's morning sun?
Later, feel the moist and struggling muscles,

> white stomach,
> old smell, peeing in my hand.

Under the weight of the fever stones
I am falling away
from the world, drifting under
the dark. I am eight,
hall voices quarrel,
". . . really sick this time,"
". . . not my fault,"
and the night ox drags me
from the last and only edge I know,
where words are the world
myself, voices
I leave up there
with my falling.

    Pull me ox, from the darkening
    hall, the white staircase,
    the attic at the farm,
    the conspiracy of dreams;
    a turtle is taking my bait,
    is beheaded; a firecracker
    has broken my little finger;
    I will lose my dog in the war;
    mama, stop sobbing in the night.
    I will not wake up.

A beach in Australia—
I emerge under sleep into a dream
surf, halftone, a color
of land where shallow salt water
stretches under the sun beyond light,
blue trees fade into yellow,
low clouds; there the chapel grows
old among moss and rain;
I hear the dark, the sounds
of the sun on the vines;
I walk beside myself
to an old time.

    Break surf, at my waist,
    my knees, my feet;
    spread out, wet sounds,
    like birds; this shadow
    leans along beaches
    and the round curve
    of land into trees
    and soft hills. Meadowing,
    I walk among buttercups with the surf
    cooling my thighs.

"The nuthatch is caping again!"

Sub-zero February noon:
a white-breasted nuthatch sways
at the feeder's edge, alone
doing that old dance
before the house of seeds—

lifting one claw
to balance on the other, softclaw;
feinting the hawthorn beak
side to side, parry-
parry, the old keep away game.

Yellow turns a bird's head
in the dead of winter: it's
the drawn sword again by the cache
in the snow—take that, juncos;
take that, chickadees and sparrows
(in the firs); "Foolsgold!"
yells a jay on a dying birch,

but keeps his distance. We, too
watch spellbound this lightheaded lasso
of two pounds of birdseed by our own
nuthatch, batty in the Thou-Shalt-Not
position under the mid-winter sun, holding
back and forth, and forth
before the glittering seeds of life.

On the Lawn of the Mental Hospital
with Susan, My Student

You could run into the woods
you say your black eyes waking
in the dope watch them
pour after you your black hair folding
over your shoulders the late afternoon clouds
bunching over the Palmer hills you list
the ordinary grievances of the loony floor Jesus
if you could only get some sleep
                        nothing
is like anything else this grass
is green your husband can come
tomorrow you will not allow the biopsy
on your breasts there are so many Susans
inside the brown mole on your cheek
you open your diary to the letter
to me sometimes you want to die so
badly that you go for days and think
of nothing else
                nothing
is like anything else John will not go
home until he finishes his jigsaw
puzzle you finish it for him
say: John you can go home now

Four Dreams, Boston, 1960

"The real effort is to stay there . . .
and examine closely the odd vegetation of
those distant regions."—Albert Camus

The lake is dry,
pale trees chalk the air.
Boulder stepping, I multiply
myself. Across the shore
a green turtle crawls
away. The sky is dead;
a seashell falls.
This cove is way inside my head.
A giant haunch frog
squats across my path:
green, solid as a maple log,
clamp mouth, grinning wrath,
drooling weeds and one green snake,
calmly gobbling up my lake.

This bridge is too high,
the other shore
too black. I'm over my
head in dark. Before
this swaying stops I'll fall.
My feet feel dead;
I've got to crawl
to keep my grip. Ahead,
the girders melt in fog
that settles at the half
way mark. This monologue
is minding every inch. My only path
is down, where waters break
the falls I take.

A deer leaps by
too close; his gray hair
musks inside my nose. I
squeeze. My gun won't fire any more.
I am tired of all
this dark head
hunting; I would call
my father, but he's dead.
And all the deer that jog
along my path
become a running dialogue
between my selves. Half
of me I hate. If I could shake
this fear, I'd lay down my gun, and
  wake.

Down through water I
struggle to a cavern floor;
a casket opens at my
knees. The light is poor,
but I begin to see all
things. What I thought was dead
becomes a jewel
shining there against red
velvet. The rest is epilogue:
myself in hand, I leave a swath
of bubbles as I rise. The surface fog
has disappeared. My old footpath
litters with old skies. I see the sun break
through for its own sake.

A Fable for My Father:
West Lebanon, Maine

"I've got nothing in the ground."
—Willy Loman

Out there in the fresh New England earth
flanked by all the different shades of green
my father planted pole beans
one by one, eye down
an inch into the ground.
Three days later he was dead.
There is a story in this.
Here it is:
       Late that night
       at the height
       of the new moon
       the ground
       cracked loud around
       the beans. No sound
       was heard until false dawn
       when a loon
       off course, circled
       the field,
       lost control,
       fell toward the poles.
       Impaled,
       it hung there like the night.

       All day the sun rode
       hot along its arc
       but no green showed.
       Just after dark
       the beans began to push;
       they came
       green gristle, lush
       up through the crack
       around the poles
       on past the loon.
       They were a growing rack

of antlers. Soon
they gouged great holes
out of the sky
and went on through
in one long lunge;
green pushed into blue.
But something had gone wrong;
the myth had reversed:
down came the giant
stalking Jack.

But these were my father's beans.
In his dreams
loomed Great East Lake
and great primeval
fish that rose to take
his bait. The wind was cool;
a duckling rose in take-off
from a pool.
He held it in his
hand. Once more
the sun was going down;
the lake was draining dry;
great gasping bullheads
lay close by
the rocks. The yellow
duck turned gray
and struggled free; it lifted
west across the bay.

The giant called
into his dream;
my father woke
and spoke my
mother's name,
"Ev,"
and then he left.

13

There was no reason
except perhaps that it was the first day
of summer—it was his favorite season.
And when he was safely in the ground
his beans came quietly up.

Processions

I just want to lie down on the Appian Way
in the sun, like an old pheasant in the off-season
forgetting shotguns and the Plymouth cold
and watch the Pines of Rome tail-feathering
green, into the sky. Under wind, the earth moves
in an ether dream, as when a building sways
for a moment, then stops. Plumage lines the sky
like Caesar coming home. Giddy with heat, my eye
whirls colors, beaded, crested, out of north
Massachusetts, white auditoriums, rainy Sundays
and the intimate ministry,
into Italy like a long-distance runner
who runs for the love of his legs
and carries no message.

Brothers, on the way home from the Olympia Theater in Lynn and the Phantom of the Opera, 1939

In the pitch-dark basement of the Methodist church
he fed the boiler to the hips:
shovel dragging in the bin, pursing his lips
against the rasp, crawling to the coal. Perched
on the piano at the other end of the room
I banged the chipped and faded keys,
giggling. Scaring myself, weak in the knees,
I hid against Jesus emerging from the tomb.

When he was inside the bin I did it again.
Roaring in the blackness, his discontent
echoed through the cold church. I measured our torment
and thundered the bass notes. I was Cain.
He was always Abel, the teen-age
janitor-organist of Lynnhurst's Dorr
Memorial. On Sunday afternoons he locked his door
and blared the Gospel Hour. In a rage

I left the house and punted a football
in Maes's field. No balls in church, only coal
and my brother's shadowed soul.
That boiler was a pig grinning at his call.
Saturday night in the fall of thirty-nine,
a white New England church: outside,
his Elgin bike and a pillow (his bribe)
and the dark, waiting for mimers who finish the mime.

Inside the bowels of that familiar place
my brother, no phantom waited
in the wings; we were scaring each other, baited
by our own opera, our own darkness,
our own faces to face.

My Cousin Dick, in the Dream

comes back. The operation
worked, he's still thirty-one
and eleven—
        the afternoon
he came to stay over: late spring, just before
supper, we bicycled down Fairmount
Avenue next to the woods, cut over
on Tom Mahan's road toward Worm
Pond. We disagreed about something
and I slapped him. He pedaled
home. I was nine. I was the little pig
in the nursery rhyme: I cried
all the way to my mother: "Dickie went home!"
She telephoned Aunt Marion
but he wouldn't come back.

Lying in bed that evening, the spring
light through the yellow window shade
filled my room with amber.
I could hear laughter
in the street: Arthur Blood
giving rides in his goat
cart. Mama let me get dressed;
when I got outside everyone
was gone. It was still light.

That spring light fills my dream. It lightens
his face. The last time I saw
him, stomping through the doorway
at the lake, laughing
toward my daughter's crib, "I want to see
the baby! I want to see the baby!"
It's still his face
trying to come through.

—Richard White, 1929-1960, his only child Richard, born six months later

Hitting Fungos in Austin, Texas

Over my left shoulder the ball smacks
into the pocket of my glove, I throw it
in, my friend bats it out,

(WHACK) the late morning sun
reddens our foreheads, our legs
range over the drydust field

playing catch (smack) as catch can
running after the southern spring, the round dove
drawing us out in the open (WHACK)

we touch each other at a hundred yards
exactly; the gray leapings
off the bat: promises

drive me back I yell drive
one over my head and we run past
noon, our bodies playing out

their turns, running over the gopher
tunnels underneath our pattering
feet, beyond Zilker Field, Texas

and our late thirties; (WHACK)
running down the old story fading
beyond my childhood glove,

running home toward an old white ball
in the sunburned grass, just beyond my
reach, sailing over my outstretched

arm, there it goes again—
I cannot run it down, I'm tired
of this long home run for now

and walk it in. The ball glistens
in my sweaty palm; I toss it in the trunk—
something to keep, between us.

Drewry's Bluff, Virginia, May 16, 1864

Item: "On the 16th (May), Beauregard attacked Butler below Drewry's Bluff and hurled him back to Bermuda Hundred Neck, where, in General Grant's expressive phrase, he 'was as completely shut off from further operations directly against Richmond as if (he) had been in a bottle strongly corked.' " —Robert E. Lee

". . . all brookies, but he didn't brighten any.
You boys are on his mind. Every night
he walks an hour before he comes to bed.
Sometimes he says it's a balmy night and worries
about the frost at the new moon. Last evening
the girls sat with us awhile but the black flies
drove us in. . . . "*

      Oozing over the bluffs, the sun
      bloodies the James. Butler stands in a daze,
      his crop is out of touch. The Red Sea dies
      in fog and silence across the woods;
      oak stumps, flayed by Minié balls,
      post guard for yesterday's and the day before yesterday's dead.
      At dark the outpost firing stops. The 8th Maine
      pickets into the fog. In the rifle pits, eyes
      burn with sour musket smoke. "Cough you bastards!
      Choke if you have to, stay awake . . ."
      Down the line, the 2nd U.S. Colored Cavalry begins
      to hum.

". . . through Littlefield's orchards. The blossoms
will be late this year. The wasps are still falling
from the eaves when the sun warms in the early
afternoon. Two old men from Kennebec drowned
in the pickerel pond last week just a ways
out from the mill. The ice gave way like cake. . . . "*

      The fog moves without wind. Wiring the wood knee-high
      the 98th New York draws outpost fire from the 8th Maine—
      they lose three men. Geese wail over the white
      and lowly night. Which way is North?

Massachusetts and Connecticut crouch on the left
and right. These stumps are telegraph poles.
How far is Maine for volunteers?

"... because of the mud. But the days are longer
now. Today it was light until quarter to five
and I stayed in the yard cutting back the raspberries.
Every year I plan to use gloves, but when I started
I was only going to clear a few. It was dark when
I finally finished. I'll soak my hands before I
go to bed. ... "

The rebel yells begin at dawn. It is a whole line
attack. The hobo columns hit and hit
the Union flank until it bleeds. The field mushrooms
in fog and smoke. At fifteen paces, muskets snap
at the looming forms. Rising for the general
retreat, the blues are cut down at the hips.
"Lee's Miserables" drag prisoners from the field
like jewels.

"... when you can. It's been a quiet spring
for us. But the ground is soaked and we're going to
plant early. This year I'm going to put morning-
glories by the side door. I'm restless to get my hands
into the warm dirt. ... "

Item. The 8th Maine Infantry Volunteers lost four officers and eighty-four men.
William and Albert Junkins, brothers, and Horace Junkins, their first cousin, were
wounded and captured. Albert was later removed to the North and deserted at
Philadelphia; he rejoined December 7, 1864, under the President's proclamation.
William died at Libbey Prison. Horace died at Andersonville.

Letter from My Father

"The summer is swiftly passing son, it is late
for the good fishing—water warm, the woods full of deer.
Mum and I just came back from a walk out to the red gate.

"Have got to go out and get some worms tomorrow for bait.
I had a box of nightcrawlers feeding on coffee grounds and beer—
the summer is swiftly passing son, it is late,

"last night a raccoon strayed under my camp and ate
all that I had. Otherwise things are pretty quiet here.
Mum and I just came back from a walk out to the red gate.

"Up on the hill today Harry and myself picked almost half a crate
of apples. We could see Wilson's Pond, the sky was so clear.
The summer is swiftly passing son, it is late,

"Everett brought down some vegetables from home, only about a plate
of peas but plenty of corn for supper. I ate four ears.
Mum and I just came back from a walk out to the red gate.

"Well boy, Alaska sounds interesting, probably our next state.
You sure got something on your dad shooting a bear.
Mum and I just came back from a walk out to the red gate,
the summer is swiftly passing son, it is late."

Robert Junkins,
Captured at Dunbar, Scotland 1650:
Died York, Maine 1699

The elms are bones in this salt June wind
and the backs of old headstones bake
in the slanting sun. Blighted birches
rattle obituaries over the graves of York.

We come as brothers in our thirties,
a Methodist minister and a college English teacher
in our Ford Falcon station wagon, our rolled white shirts
and our family genealogy, plotting old graveyards
that square the sloping hills of Scotland Parish
on the Berwick Road. Ten generations
of grass re-claim the sunk and beveled sod:
leaves packed in, slates underground. We read,
"the place of his burial is not of record,"
and stand on stained and crumbly bricks
where the Junkins Garrison stood for 230 years. Stickweed
and briars gather the old names. Further up the hill
a new house with a pack of screaming dogs
leaping to the ends of their chains: York, Maine 1963.

We wonder who we are. Across the undergrowth,
heat snakes from the black macadam; old John
McIntyre's reconstructed garrison wavers against the sky.
Down the sloping fields, brown grass beds,
scuffles to the wind; the Bass River
meanders under dunes of hay. (No English soldiers camp
these soft and brine-ruffed slopes, no horses
scream from the gashes of pikes.) The bones that chalk
this ground are Scots' bones; the winds
inside our own skulls blow north.

The name *Junkins* sticks with us. Cromwell's
cannon at the Bar of Doon still surrounds it. Here
among the scatterbrush and half-buried bricks
we read the *Old Parliamentary History*
and think about names. Did Robert John-kin
bargain for another life? —an eight-day march
without food: scavenging rotten cabbages

at the Morpeth Gardens, men falling
like poisoned bugs, marching to the Bishop's
Castle where physicians let blood—
A Scot sold for thirty pounds in London,
then he was shipped to the sawmills
in the New World. Robert, John-kin.

We watch the leaves drift across the family plot
inter-boned with slate and granite
slabs. Our shovel unearths a few grays
and reds. What we are is already in the ground.
These falling leaves will pack us in.

On this bright June day with the wind at our backs
we walk together to the car.
Each of us carries an old red brick.

Item: At the battle of Dunbar, 8100 Scots were killed or wounded by Cromwell's army. Of the 3900 prisoners who were force-marched to London, more than half died on the way; the remainder were sent to the coal mines and the salt works or sold into indenture in America. For the march, Cromwell assured their escort, Hesilrigge, Governor of Newcastle, "I know you are a man of business."

After the Six a.m. Phone Call about
the Fire Headed for Great East Lake,
We Drove from Saugus in the '38 Buick

and watched the smoke redoubling
at the other end of the lake
            across the cove the Shaws
backed a truck down and were filling it
with furniture

the water was so low
we could have walked around the shore
there won't be nothing left for a mile
around he said
behind us on the hill we could hear
the Pearsons loading
the old man yelled she's a boiling
plenty plenty boys

boys boys the echo came across
the water
we must have stood there for ten
minutes and never said a word
then Uncle Norman hurried down
the hill and called hi Ralph it
don't look none too good they
say it's blistering houses a quarter-
mile away

he went inside and got a bed
going up the hill with the mattress
on his back he said Esther and I
had a lot of good times on this
and drove back to North Berwick

my father and I watched on the shore
another half-hour   it was the only time
I ever saw him at the lake
in his General Electric foreman's
clothes

and he said what do you say boy
if it goes
                  it goes
there won't be nothing left
for a mile around

so we walked up the hill empty-
handed to the long ride
home and our separate
autumn ways

Autumn in Georgia

Gone into the lists of horror
after the fact, swamp standing, knee-deep in the maggot pudding,
blear-eyed, scurvied, stunned,
feces dribbling down their legs,

the Catholic priest, his white linen coat darkened
by vermin, crawling beside bodies
burrowed into the earth for confession,
the sky rippling with heat over the blue rags
clutching tiny sacks of unbolted meal
(at Libby they ate the commandant's poodle),
intestines etched by husks;

after the Maine lakes sloshed in the vague and drying
memories, the dragged entrails,
delirium, bugs crawling on the dying faces
too weak to chew crackers,

after the hope of Providence Spring
and "Boston" Corbett leaping praises for the miracle god
(he survived to kill John Wilkes Booth),
the three thousand dead in August
hauled away by the Negro Federals each morning;

after the loss of light.

There is a brook in Kennebunk, Maine
runs through the mind, called "Branch"
where the alders tangle and the brookies
mean and sweet find their way to the Little Sandy
in the woods behind Webber's farm.

—Horace Junkins, born September 1831, Hollis Maine;
died Andersonville Prison, September 1864

A Remembrance: Chadbourne Hall, 1949, A Three-Cent Jefferson Stamp Brings a Letter from My Father

---

". . . last week end I was up to Pop's gunning
but didn't see anything or didn't hear a shot all day . . ."

That picture Thelma Hutchins took
in her living room the night before
you died is leaning on a book
here on my desk. I see it more

now that I've bought some land
down on the Maine coast, and a boat
to boot. Thirty years ago when we clammed
the flats of the York River you used to quote

your own father: "Live off the sea
as near as you can." The time we fried
some in corn meal just to see
how they'd be that way, you tied

us all in knots laughing about
how they were as tough as her pecan
pie. (You bought that cottage without
telling her from the other Hutchins who ran

the country store in North Berwick,
Bertha White's father.) You used to crawl
underneath every spring with a red brick
and the car jack to raise the corner level

a couple inches where the stilts had sunk
in the puddle slime. One Sunday afternoon
late in summer, the flood tide up to the trunk
of the car, we sat in the front seat marooned

with the radio and a Red Sox
double-header. We heard Williams hit
his thirty-sixth. When real estate went up, the clock
stopped on all that. You sold out, quit

29

Wells Beach forever. We drove each weekend
to the lake and trolled for white perch
into the evening dark. Rowboats of friends.
We tacked up the rotogravure, birch

trees, strippers, hunters and dogs.
And penny ante games by lantern light,
water lilies and pickerel in the boat, frogs
at dusk, the whippoorwill at nine each night—

She sold the camp last summer, I brought
the deer head home. The outside pump
had rusted out. Uncle Harry said he thought
he saw the wood stove at the dump.

That part of it is gone too. Tonight
I re-read your letter the first year I
was gone: "Well Boy, you sure had quite
an experience. How is your injury

coming along?" Not even the fog
can bring it all back. What sticks
in my mind now is that grassy bog
at the end of the narrows in the second lake, thick

with river bass. I startled a nesting loon
on a quiet summer day. That yodeling shriek
got me to the oars. I rowed all afternoon.
That old bird knew how to speak

of quiet, and the passing of time, and the young
leaving home. I have two boys myself now
and a daughter. They will know us both among
firs and the morning tide. That's a vow.

It All Ends Up in the
Backyard Encounter with the Cock

There once was a little red hen
Her name was Henny-Penny Pen
She turned into a rooster.
Cock-a-doodle do!

August 1939

This killing was no Sunday morning decapitation
between the birdbath and the garage: I stood
as quiet as a quiet child, watching
my uncle use three hatchet cuts to chip
the head off and fling the leaking ruff
of feathers to the grass so I could watch
the headless spree around the yard. "There he goes!
There he goes!" he said. But it was only chicken
little. It fell in a clump, primed its wings
three times, as if to test its death, and quieted.
"Pluck! Pluck! Pluck!" we said, and ducked
the feathery thing in boiling water
and the blood sinned off in curls. This
was no nightmare in magenta. This was Sunday dinner.

A Dream, 1958

The dove winds down its journey
into oils, and blue spins on itself
as if the sun is rooming in,
there! —the Barbary cock!

October 1924

Big with my brother, my mother walked
the backyard path down toward the cemetery
wall, away from Ontario Street. At her feet
the brood of Plymouth Rocks clucked
when flash the talons spurring in her face
wings beating against her
"Ralph! Ralph!" she called

feathers pounding against her face her breasts
her swollen belly "Ralph! Ralph! Oh dear God, Ralph!"
My father pulled the raging cock away
and flung it, swan-like, in a muscle burst
thirty feet across the garden where it fluttered
against the dirt, hitched, tested its wings
and crowed. All that was left
for each of them was to stare.

A Dream, 1958

Near the unfamiliar barn the chickens prattle
in the grain. In this black and white
only the cock is color. Stark, autumnal,
sheen, he magnifies himself. My gunsight
withers to a pin. The cock moves into the brood again—
from my side I reach my hands
and feel the comb, the breast, the fiery
neck. My feathers preen in the warmth.
He holds me to the beating of his heart.
In hand, I flesh my feathers to a hush
and crow my only song to the spiraling
dawn.

Postscripts to a Childhood

The cows have all come home
now, but the cowbells hollow
in the dusk, and the old farm
hovels quietly. A swallow
flies from the loft of the torn-down
barn in Kennebunk, Maine.

Before the thyroid killed
him and he watched me from
the empty room, in dreams
I rode a stallion
down an old dirt road where a team
of oxen carted him
again into my head: my
father. The cow
that gored him in the thigh
that Sunday morning I
was five and miles away
in Sunday school with coloring
books, returned one night
when I was twenty-eight
and gored his head.

I was miles away
again; they phoned to tell
me, and the cowbells
runkled in the West.
I stood there like a drummer
with no drums, and then
I dressed and cried and drove
into the sun
which was a dove
on the first day of summer.

Blacksnaking to Pine Grove
the coffin-cuddled hearse wove

like a serpent's head to the family lot
and waited in the sun—a plot
of ground still walking distance from the house
where he grew up. He shot grouse
there as a boy before the graveyard
ate up the woods and the ground starred
with veteran's flags. He fished for bass
in Holder's Pond, boiled sassafras
roots in water; once he stole a hen,
nicked off its head with a pen-
knife, and roasted it with the feathers on.

Hopping rocks to Black Eagle Swamp
and beanpoles, he stopped before his longest jump
when a six-foot blacksnake, sunning
hissed him backwards, sent him running
home. He said he didn't dare go back: "Those beanpoles are still there."

> *Those woods you named as yours are gone;*
> *you are lying in that ground*
> *all unaware. Not a hound*
> *dog in the world could trace*
> *you out. The chase*
> *is over now; you disappear*
> *within your woods like an antler*
> *shed in June. Those ducks*
> *wheeling in like low line drives*
> *can find no water anywhere. They cruise*
> *off course, like bees from broken hives*
> *whose queen is occupied with fallen fruit; she sucks*
> *the rotting apple on its bruise.*

Recoiling back to sandwiches and relatives
we ride the seven-seated Cadillac with Dives;
we pass a swimming pool and hear small children shout;
we are insiders looking out
from close and huddled clover.
A strange rehearsal is over.

In the other woods a fox
quickens in the sunlight on a hill;
a hen leads baby woodcocks
through moist grass to where the pines are still.

The Inheritance

"I Lydia Junkins Widow of York"
it begins. Before witnesses,
before the eyes loll to the brine
old January sky and memory
drifts in the marsh grass
to the sea that will not freeze;
the only evidence is will.

She makes no bones
and dispenses with it all. You, Susan Junkins,
hark, she names you first of eight:
"one brass kittle one Churn and four flat Irons
one half of my bedding one Great Chair
all my Chairs one blue Chest
and the remainder of the bed clothes to do as please—"

As please you Susan.
As please us all. Wheezy, diminutive,
stark, she measures out her life
and fades, an old impersonation.
We are on our hands and knees in the cellar
stacking old magazines. Idling, we thumb through pages
and the smell of the past. We remember windows that open
over great fields to the sea. Our breasts ache
after the wind.

She names the names.
John H. Junkins, second: "I give to him
the great Bible and one half of a bed—"
and down the list.
Leonard: "The Clock and one half of a bed—"
Lydia: "one bed"
Susan E. and Aba: "one bed"
Henry, Charlotte Foster and Mary M: "one pair
of sheets and one pair of Pillow Cases."
And then it is over with
the bank book and the children
divisible, apportioned, willed.

We receive the past by decree.
Our portions weigh in our seasoning hands.
From York, we are given Lydia X her Cross.

—Lydia Junkins, 1769–1856

"Ten years from now you'll walk these woods alone"

he said, crossing a rise on the edge
of the second lake, the smell of the hot October
woods profound, slash piles from old loggings all around
us whitening, settling in the hot October ground.
I, embarrassed, angry, turned away.
That was twenty years ago
I knew what I knew
I knew my father day by day

A squirrel hunt was a squirrel hunt.
My mind was set on shooting a big gray
(I learned to name the names from him)
He said it's the getting out here
and sitting down and waiting that does it
stepping over a dead birch
snapping off a dead branch so it wouldn't snap
across my face, you can search
for hours but you won't walk up on a big gray.
That was twenty years ago
I knew what I knew
I knew my father day by day

We'll find ourselves a good big oak
and wait he said (the wind and sun all tangled
in the trees) before you know it the birds'll rustle
in the leaves. We sat. Try not to move a muscle
now, and by and by a fat old gray will show
along a limb, or move across the leaves.
At every sound I froze. It's him. It's him.
It's the fat old gray.
That was twenty years ago
I knew what I knew
I knew my father day by day

Then the gray moves soft along the ground
and stops. Just squeeze he barely whispered
in my ear just line him up—he lifts an acorn
he's just found, my finger gives away

the sound, the woods part gray fur kicking
quiet down the gun bolt warm inside my thumb—
how the squirrel calms the woods. That's good
shooting son he said laying in my hand
the fat old gray.
He died ten years ago himself
What he knew he couldn't say
I knew my father day by day.

"Look—it's a purple finch!"

A glimpse of backwoods color
by the outer kitchen door
quickens our winter landscape
with certain things, and more—

this quiet visitor
in dyestuffs
closest to the heart
among pinegreen, hillblue—

perspective in the foreground,
January art: more
than strapling maples
black brooming the darkening sky—

what gives distance distance:
tint of raspberry
in the snow—
so close, we know.

3 May Fairfield, Harry White, and Henry Thoreau

May Fairfield

She slept one night of her sixty-seventh year
with a dead husband.
Rolling against cold flesh at dawn
she drew away
as if shying back from a crater,
then waited,
and gathered her mind.

After the autumn Yankee funeral
where he lay old and shiny
like crackle-glaze ceramic,
May Fairfield sat with guests,
accepted a ride to the base of her hill
and walked upward, home.
Shucking corn for supper,
the night rain mulched the ground with husks.

With the excuse of Christmas
she spun presents on her loom
for neighbors who sucked the muddy hill with boots
and carried store-bought goods.
Standing in her ninety-seven pounds
she smiled, when asked, and dragged a shotgun
from her bedroom.
"What have I got to be afraid of?"
Later that summer she confided,
"I sneak down to the brook
and get myself a trout when I want one."

Two years ago, May Fairfield perched
in my mother's kitchen and ate half a piece of Johnny-cake
while the cattails fluffed into the sky
and leafed the fowling clouds.
She told how she ate six times a day now
since the cancerous half of her stomach
was cut out like a rotten gourd.

She never mentioned his muscling shoulders
reaching up with forks of hay
and her stamping on the springy pile,
his pipe thoughts exhaled on an autumn night,
his breaths wheezed out across an armful
of sunrise winter oak,
his nighttime touch;
nor did she tell of that awful morning,
how she was cold inside
as if suddenly walking into a lowland fog.
She showed my mother the iron she spun
from her veins into seven aprons,
two tablecloths, and a comforter.

That October, she sat by her window
knitting for Christmas. For something that afterwards
she forgot, she shuffled to the kitchen.
A crashing filled her head and noise
shivered through the rooms.
Some fool hunter flushed a partridge by her barn
and shot it flying past her window.
Glass spit at the corners and onto the shelves.
She told us she crept to the window
and waited for him to dare and fetch his bird.
Two hours later, while the sun set like melting steel
she went out and fetched it herself
and plucked it, and cooked it, and ate it.

May Fairfield knitted through December
but wrote mother that she couldn't keep warm
even though she kept a fire in all three stoves
with wood the lumberjacks tossed
in her shed last fall.
"I wouldn't let them split it though," she wrote,
" 'Split it myself,' I told them," and added,
"I nicked my leg once, but it healed."

In February, a neighbor out rabbit hunting
found May Fairfield in the woodshed
frozen to the floor like a brush bough
after a heavy frost.
She was curled up in four homemade woolen
sweaters, and held an axe half through a piece of oak.

That spring a lawn auctioneer
bellowed away the Fairfield farm in the rain,
and the Methodist church bought the loom at $1.77
for the missionary sewing circle.

Uncle Harry: Basin View, 1936

from the cove, rowing back
alone, the mid-morning sun drying
the pickerel strewn under the seats
of his flat-bottomed boat

finishing it off, trolling almost
to the tie-tree, adrift now
reeling in, he spits out the last inch
of his cigarette: get any I ask

thirty-three summers ago, those black
pickerel jaws stiffening in the hard gator
slouch. naryaone he grins
throwing them one by one at my feet

clambering up the bank to the fish
table: edging his knife beneath
the stumplimp necks, thumbing down the blade
stripping the skins like masking tape

Uncle Harry at the Fish Table,
Great East Lake, 1940

never mind scraping scales,
you got to get the skins
off.
Norman showed up one weekend
with his new way: slabbing
them skins on, slicing the meat
from the skin—but I told him
it's mean on your fingers, and wasteful

   slice a little
forward behind the gills on both
sides to the backbone and break it
so's you won't dull your knife; slit
backside and belly
to the tail—keep the back
of the blade
flat against the backbone, and cut

hard along the bone itself; you
can strip the slabs clean—
here, you take these
up to your mother and tell her
put them in the icebox

Uncle Harry: Shooting Partridge, 1941

the yellow farmhouse over Wilson's Pond way
he said to meet; go through
the strip lot up top of the ridge
and bear right; there's a young juniper

pasture in there and a grown-over road
that comes out to the old red gate
where your father shot the doe last year;
I've put up birds in there;

go easy near the alder
swamp; might be two or three
in a clump; if one goes up way off
circle around; don't hurry none,

they're a cagey bird; might wait
till you go by and flush up
right behind you; you got to
fire high in a thicket; if they get

room they'll stay low; lead 'em
good; look up going through
pines; they'll perch in the dead
limbs. Then we left off together.

Working off that other ridge he said
he jumped a red fox and headed
into the orchard. I met him later, grinning,
gun slung over one arm, pockets bulging with apples.

Uncle Harry: Splitting Oak
before Pickerel Fishing, 1942

the way he said
it moving his thumb just
enough before the axe

tossing both
pieces at the pile:
I heard they was a fire
in the bed this morning
then he left it alone and kept on
with the wood
in one hand, the axe in
the other, cracking it apart, now
and then smelling the grain
(that morning
I had wet the bed, and skipped
breakfast)
when they yelled over did I want
anything to eat he had two or three days
fall burning in the pile

out on the water he talked low:
just skip the belly along
like this
now   one's got it
see there?   we'll just sit and wait
till he chews it. You've got
to let them chew it. See his jaws
working? Pretty soon the belly'll be
gone. He'll have the whole thing
in his mouth. Then you can set
the hook. It just takes time.

Uncle Harry at the Woodpile, Great East Lake, 1948

one arm against a pine at his side
door looking at the lake pushing a soft
boiled egg into his mouth full
his false teeth in his pockets gumming

the words god damn it my father standing
there grinning have them out you
said you'll feel better I can't eat
a god damn thing wiping his chin glancing

at me he picks up his axe and works
his kindling pile the three of us
not saying a word the pine boards
snapping apart his left hand holding

the ends just over the edge
of the chopping block the axe catching

each end turning the pile grows
a breeze blows up on the lake
I can smell bread baking inside our camp
hear the boats scrape against

the rocky shore he finishes
with the pine kindling and starts
on the oak, every now and then picking
a piece, feeling the smooth cut

        starting a new pile
the only thing he said to me
in two hours: fall'll be here
pretty quick

Walden, 100 Years after Thoreau

July

The clouds were fishbone
high. Downwind.
From the pond
water color rose toward the sun
like heat, and voices
carried from a boat.
Four feet from shore
two executive bass
meandered by,
bored by bait
and waiting.

     Armed,
a crawfish backed
from underneath a rock;
a boy amused his girl
by skipping stones
across the cove;
a lone Canada goose
dove under; some cloven crows
flapped out of a pine
like a frayed black bow
untying.

Summer had closed
in. At dusk
the waterfront began
to clear; tiptoeing
bathers crossed the gravel
to their cars. Kibbies
cupped their noses
up for flies and
popped the watertop. A band
of blacks with a banjo
settled in.

The smell
of warm fresh water
wafted toward the shore;
across the cove where
Thoreau built his
hut, seventy frogs
were bulling:
"chug-a-rum,
chug-a-rum."
The night was opening
like a cotyledon.

October

The wind is up. Clouds
bulge over like amoebas,
as if White's Pond
were giving up its ghosts. Down
on the water, a boat with fishermen
drifts too close, and two gulls
change their spot; a walker
circles the edge of the pond
doing his legwork, like Truman;
polliwogs motor from the shallows,
headfirst.

From the west shore, dead pines
loll over the water
like paws; buff cattails
sway in back of the cove; two darning
needles alight on a rock—
scared by the wind, they dart
straight up, as quick as pickerel,
chase each other, mate,
sag toward the water,
release. A boy and his date
plop acorns from the beach, and laugh.

Juniper and butternut are in the air,
maple leaves scatter on the ground
like peaches. Overhead,
a bomber jets her orange nose
toward Hanscom Field.
The water is unruffled,
thistledown drifts lazily,
like air.
Two young people and their daughter
walk slowly to the site of Thoreau's hut
and back.

On the vacant public beach
white swimming buoys are strung out
in the sun. Near the water
a crawfish shell turns blue,
a father and his little boy
are sailing a boat.
From the hill behind,
snowfence shadows lengthen
toward the sand; across the pond
a Buddliner hustles by. Out on Route 2
cars are roaring east and west.

January

From the commuter train
window, you only glimpse
in six seconds
the whiteness of the ice,
several pinholes,
a fisherman on one knee,
and a small fire on the shore.
Then the pond is gone
and the trees are going by,
then a swamp, then a field,
and you are in Lincoln.

You lift your paper again
to read. But back at the pond
the fisherman sees a red flag
go up, walks to the trap,
leisurely retrieves his trout
and lays it in the square well
that he hand-chipped in the ice.
The trout stabilizes itself
in the cold water, as if it
lay in a pool
of Novocain.

Later, more fishermen appear
in ones and twos, and skaters
criss-cross the rumbling ice.
A fat woman drags her son
on a sled. A hockey game
starts up. The wind is still.
Down a hundred feet
the currents are so strong,
divers, looking for bodies,
have surfaced,
refusing to go back.

Lying on his belly,
Thoreau used to peer
down through a hole
in the ice, staring
into the water until
the cold drove him
back to his warm cabin.
It was just the being there
over all that depth that got him
like an eagle looking down
from two miles up.

April

On the morning
before opening day
there was a threat
of rain. Trout
broke to the calm
without sound
and the spread of circles
grew; the pond
was cold
and quiet; birches
held steady as Dalmatians.

On the point
from the west cove
I imagined with my fisherman's eye
a line into each disappearing
wake;
underwater
forms idled in the depths
of this green and gray
and mist-blown book.

I was the only one
at the pond; a nervous
chipmunk
hurried in the leaves;
on a wooden marker
pointing to the stones
at the site of Thoreau's hut
a solitary bluebird
waited; two Canada geese,
necks arching, swam into the cove
peering like serpents.

I stayed for an hour.
When the first drops
began to fall, I followed
the path back,
past the empty picnic benches,
the slough, the signs
to the vacant fire lane.
The wet pine spills were as quiet
as moss,
and the rain
rained down in praise of all ponds.

4   To the Coast

Antelopes

Driving across Wyoming at sunset
at the end of the fifth day from the Atlantic,
the children asleep, the engine cooling toward normal,
the trailer fiery and orange in the evening calm
at the bidding of my foot, like the past (except for childhood)
we passed antelopes that hesitated toward the black road before dusk
and lifted from their grazing to watch our passing

and those faces, those studies in browns and blacks in the softening
sun, the quiet bodies, the energy of neck and eye
agile in their wild and tentative curiosity,
becalmed and motionless before our raging, dying speed
the figures in their brooding heads adding always to zero
confident in the economy of form, and fear
and flight,

emerge from canvas, and yellow clouds, and sagebrush
rolling among soft winds into oil and color and prairie
beyond gunshops and sports magazines, or someone's trophy den
to the real staring faces, sentinels from the Old West
who watched prairie schooners like old habits
among women crazy for the rush of the ocean in their ears
and lay down after eating in the cool desert dark,

who watched us cruise toward that other West
beyond the now dark evening sky, beyond the Wasatch,
beyond ourselves and Shoshoni, Wyoming, where we slept.

Distances

huddling on Friday afternoons
on a corner of the girls' vacant athletic field
the old athletes play out their lives

> *under the peeling*
> *sycamores we throw*
> *our passes*

running
on imaginary lines

nearby
their young sons wander off
unconcerned from the corners
of their eyes they watch
a simpler game,
distance

> *our partridge*
> *pulses pound*
> *under the wind*
> *we long to punt*
> *oh to loft that*
> *lovely ball beyond*
> *the trees*
> *where there are no ends*
> *grids hands*
> *that stop one*
> *cold with touch*

here all passes
for practice

> *the ball strides through*
> *the air lacings*
> *loom our gamey hearts*
> *consume us*

at dusk they gather sons
and swagger toward the lockers
and their wives

the fall is in the air

The Letter

*"the remains were those of Mr. James C. White . . . slipped while coupling cars,
the whole train of fifteen cars and the engine passing over his body, scattering
and dragging the remains up and down the tracks . . . gathered up in coal-hods and
taken to the baggage room."*
—from a Portsmouth, Maine newspaper, 1868

In this offhand news from the East
New England is that old child stirring in my sleep.
You enclose my child-poem in red ink
(your old Christmas list penciled on the back)
and a tattered clipping of our great-grandfather's
death.

I read the old news again. Out on the patio
my two boys vroom vroom with their trucks.
Their middle names ring with the past.

I read that the engineer saw a piece of a man's head
by the track. I read our child handwriting
in red and black, and watch the gnomes
scurrying off with our lives.
Only rooms remain.

> *dodge-ball, dodge-ball . . . gorgons all around*
> *ring-a-leavey-o . . . red light, red light,*
> *kick the can . . . all-ee all-ee infree*

In the kitchen of gramma's house
I sit in my chair beside the coal-hod.
Dandelion greens, salt pork, potatoes
simmer on the stove. In the cold living room
Aunt B's fingernails click
on the ivory keys. Outside
in the backyard, the garden
stops at the cemetery wall.

> *My lost moccasins*
> *walk at Bauneg Beg. The beads glisten under water.*
> *The yellow hopscotch of the undershell*

turtles in my hands. I feel the claws.
I ask are you going to cut off his head.
For a book the blood pours into broth.

When daddy was lowered into the ground
mama wailed, "Daddy, daddy, I didn't want you to die."

   Picking picking at my covers after dark.
   The family worries beside the bed; no one
   can comfort me.
   Later I fumble on the windowsill for the door
   and wake beneath your bed.

You say everyone is well.
The leaves are turning at the farm.
In the mornings, deer nibble under the apple tree.
Your dog Caesar is getting deaf.
You have left the church.

We can only list the past.
The trolls, our old selves
back down in the end.
Long ago we were all in free.

The Beach at Hyannisport, Late November 1963

The winter Atlantic slams Cape Cod
a month early. The hurly burly's done again,
dark pink shows in the southern sky.
The president's wife holds
the president's broken head, and lets go.
She lets us let go here. Breakers falling
on the beach rush in, rush back
into the undertow.

"He looked at me with that beautiful
quizzical look, and died."

Walking near surf, gathering rose hips,
moving on. Voices in the wind
are the wind itself. Jellyfish
lie at our feet, stopped cold by frost.

> *The fretting waves, pines*
> *mayflowers, flakes on the empty beach*
> *quiet. The Charles and the Potomac sleep.*
> *Jefferson and Lee, stones.*
> *Families divide the sea light,*
> *the night earth.*
> *Dead children reach.*

The beach: quiet except for wind and surf.
Sandpipers run, jab the foam.

> *A horse stumbles, goes down in the waves.*
> *Gulls flash across the coffin-corner*
> *of the sky.*

The wind is strange, the west dark.
The last wild roses bend to the wind.
A rib has gone from our side.

Going

---

floating in inner
tubes bumping the creek
bed down
stream passing

a whole day before
my flight

our oldest on her
own waving up
                ahead

the great
oaks over
us the creek
bending vines
hanging

     our buttocks
bumping rapids
easing into deep
water each
holding another
son

doubled now
moving a-
part this
boy I touch
was born

     in con-
cord mass-
achusetts then

      the black
      o's double
      floating that

boy you
arm to you
now
born three
thousand miles
a-
      way
here
this park
this and that
life here
I

am you
are they
are
come
with me

      together
      again
      the black inner
      tubes

I asked you
said again
your face
falling
down your
crying
head I

can't
move
away

      drifting
we saw

our little
girl
      there
      floating

still
moving up
ahead

Daniel, My Son

Now in the waning of my thirty-third year
you weigh in my arms against the sky
a young lamb, unshorn, lean
in your arms and kicking legs. I
toss you up to the maple leaves,
to the sky, the day moon
and tomorrow. Quick and true, dear son,
each time you plummet straight to the heart.

For you are three,
and will not remember me
in the dark of your fitful dreams,
your innocent cribbage.
I tell you now,
my fingers shall feel your brow
in all our days and nights
be the moon over the trees
or down.

We named you Daniel
for yourself. Little scrambler,
honey boy, you twist your happy tongue
into our twisted hearts (you
say *bitch* for *fish*, *die-ee*
for *daddy*).
You are the sunfish and the sandman
of our love. You have fallen away
from my genitals like a star.

Karn, All Hallow's Eve, 1965

Last night we carved your pumpkin
gristle clean, before I walked out
for good, or ill.
Spooning the yellow cobwebs,
your brother eyed
the bone-white seeds,
but you are six. You know the in's
and out's of life. You cried.

Tonight hobgoblins walk the streets
with chaperones. Somewhere you shuffle
in the dark; you hold your pumpkin
as the world's last light. Blackened,
darkened, you scare yourself.

Little crone, my heart's sprout,
if you could tap my exile door tonight
I'd shout "Trick!"
and bare my breast, eyes closed,
for kindred hands to carve
my pumpkin soul.

Somewhere, grimacing triangles,
you are facing the dark. My dear,
the dead are all around you,
and our empty breathing
cannot dim your heart's
light.

Theodore, among the Skylarks

"I have watered the red huckleberry, the sand cherry, and the nettle tree, the red pine and the black ash, the white grape and the yellow violet, which might have withered else in dry seasons."
—Henry Thoreau

Little groundhog, scurrier of kittens,
tromper of flowers, terrorizer of bookshelves,
climber of all things that go up,
your domain is light and air.
Sitting in sinks like a Buddha
you are our burl of love.

Our youngest son,
for eighteen months you have taught us
the wages of love. You are our good throw
of the dice, our three for three.

My lovely boy, I hear you breathing
everywhere in all my nights,
your pursing lips
a treasure for the dark.

On this last night,
this fall in the curve
of seven years,
I place my jewel in your tightening fist.

The Top of the Fairmont, March 1965

It is Saturday afternoon in the Crown Room;
our whiskey sours are yellow, orange, red.
Down there the pastel city spreads
our tablecloth, our spring picnic,
our ride down the velvet valley from ourselves
and seven years.

In the morning we walked.
We chose Union Street; west of Van Ness the tar-stained
houses lumbered with the state of Maine. Black lobsters.
In the gardens, azaleas burned in the morning sun.
A gallery, a shop, a quaint doorway
and the ocean air—the air of New England afternoons
in October: bicycling through Gloucester,
walking from a football game in Woburn,
those burning Lynnhurst leaves.
A child's life is in the air.

Up here the Victorian green softens above the bay;
white clouds cotton to the wind.
There, the hill telegraphs darkness,
there the sun lazars through the clouds.
It could all be treasure.
The wild deer are swimming through the Golden Gate.

On the morning of the day the moose came to Amherst

I was addressing three air mail cards
in the post office across from Ashley's Garage
when I heard a voice behind the cage:
"That moose is sure causing a stir in town."

"What moose?" I asked casually, keeping my head down.

"Over there on Market Hill
Road. Fred Ruder's pasture.
Right in with some heifers.
Red antlers and all.
There's a big crowd over there."

I dropped my postcards in the slot.
"Sometimes they like to move around a lot."

"This one likes cows, they say.
Came all the way over from the Quabbin.
Forest service put him there last week.
They painted his antlers red so's they could track him.
He came over the Pelham Hills in one day."

So I drove over
to see the moose
with red antlers
        who likes cows.

It was an overcast September day.
Maples flushed the pasture's edge.
Cars lined nose to rear along the Ruder's hedge.
New cloth signs wrapped every other tree:
"No Hunting, Fishing, Trespassing."
Calmly the moose stood among the cows.
Small crowds held cameras by the fence.
They joked, testing the barbed wire
and hailed a Quaker with a camera-gun:
"Blessed are the meek, Trevor."

I heard a lady ask the forest service man,
"Is it true he's full of tranquilizers?"

"I been watching this moose for a week.
He's as sober as you are."

"I heard they're going to bring over a cow moose
for him."

"Where the hell are we going to get a cow moose?"

After a while I drove my car
home, and ate lunch
        and fell asleep.

When I awoke it was raining.
On the porch I watched a daddy longlegs
walk up the inside of the screen.
I flicked my thumb beneath it and it stopped.

        "You may take no giant steps,"
        my little girl used to call.

I imagined it walking to California in the fall
like a great spider moose,
lounging over the Great Plains,
stepping over mountains,
my sons running wide-eyed
into the house, as after a sonic boom.
Outside, the wind came up, and the rain stopped.

One purple thistle was still in bloom;
the rest were white, and ghosted in the air.
My hands grew cold.
I began a letter to my four year old:
        "Dear son. Today I saw a moose.
        He was a fine moose. He walked over a hill
        from a lake, to be friends with some cows.
        He had red horns, and he came to my town.

I didn't touch him because he was too big,
but he was fun to look at. He stood around
watching, having a nice time. When it rains
he probably goes under a tree, or in a barn.
Mummy tells me that you play a game with scarves
at nursery school. When you have a red one
you can be a moose, and the other kids
can be cows. And everybody will be friends."

I heard the wind grow fiercer in the trees.
Leaving my letter and the chilling room
I walked the woods
past the brook, past the cabin
that is falling down
to the field with the black and white cows.
Below the rattling of the leaves
they stood, and lay, and ate like nuns
under vows of silence.

I watched from a rock until the sun
set below the Hadley Hills,
and thought of giant steps, and scarves,
and the coming of the snow.

     "Don't go, daddy, don't go."

When the cows started back
I followed along the barbed wire,
then cut through the woods to the house.
The hardwood twigs cracked
beneath my feet.

In the empty living room
I piled old limbs,
old antlered bones,
     and built a fire.

Popponesset Beach,
August 1967

and sandpipers you
said walking
from the beach changing
the subject the scrub pines
cooling still
toward our rented
cottage
      where he came
that afternoon gobbling
pills to your soft no
reciting letters wobbling
on the hot sand your
brother easing
him toward the Mustang

they see everything you
said touching
my arm I've never
seen them running
as scared as they ran
today
      on the beach
      your mother said men
      scare me
on the dead
run water cocks
         legging it
the surf seething
at their feet

he just fell all apart you
said changing
the subject again touching
my arm I've never seen
that before
      the children
trailing golden
beach towels

| 75

behind us water
Scots   jackdaws

bag pipers their bellies
salt on our mouths later

Your Coming

moving as you
do those things
around the room
moving as you

touch the children
breathing in their
rooms of things
alive geraniums

in an iron pot coming
to life cedar
trees outside
the window moving

as you make our
life a Kirman
rug chrysanthemums
moving yellow

rust the past now
grape juices our mouths
our hands clusters
on antique chairs

moving as you
touch the moist earth
iris crocus tulip
bulbs a house

our yard woods
moving yes
yes now
your breasts

yes trees rooms
stop everything
moving as you
do

Poaching Blue-Eyed Scallops
at Lake Coskata, Nantucket

here we are calmly
wading after
eight years
        the four of us four
        children later
        wading
bending all eight
of us picking
        knee
deep the water
rising these lovely
hinges twenty sapphires
apiece
        retinas
attached we fill
the floating bucket
        exclaiming
over each
one
        occasionally
        clacking in our palms false
        teeth

that party eight
years ago on the main-
land the four
of us
        (children)
jockeying through
the night passing
out-
        side the same
ocean crashing
remarkably
apart
        from our lives crashing
always within
earshot

we do not speak
of it
now the calm
tide coming in and out
there the waves crashing
the summer sun
going

     we finish collecting
our children growing
cold we wrap sweatshirts
         over them
riding the fenders past
         the samphire past
         the bayberry
and the beach
plums over
and over the sand
thinking of eight
years moving in

the dark
toward wauwinet

Somewhere on Madaket Shore, the Anniversary of our Reconciliation

the fog horns
in the damp
air moving doors
   over
these dunes blowing
from the ocean full
      of certain
parts

of speech crashing
a little
way beyond
   the both of
us the whiteness
out

     there
across the sound
bringing
our bodies again
and again old shells
beach
grass rose
hips somewhere

  nearby
you are sketching bay
bushes
in the hooded terrycloth
robe we found
in the drawer
   of that big
house

quiet-
  ly darkening in
the spaces

For Robert Kennedy:
Sunderland, June 8, 1968

Moving back
and forth between
my beans
and the day long
news

yellow
colors lean
toward the closeness
and the intermittent
rain:
       dandelions (my young
         son calls the minor
         ones cubs)

flowering wild
strawberries in our uncut
grass
the first
lemon lilies among the ground
grapes

traveling from the edge
of the woods
to the woods
itself

Something is tearing
up my
garden
a small selection
of diggings into
the corn
strewn

strays, the squash
hills thrown

open
tombs, the white
sides of
        seeds scattered
like car doors

a few butter
beans just bare-
ly through
knocked over
            periscopes

Junkins' vegetable
junkyard

Not everything
succumbed
to the paw-
        ing

young asparagus
pickerels
up among the ordinary
weeds
green antennae
grounded

in my own
garden
the grief
is just
as deep

5 Crossing by Ferry

Crossing by Ferry

Out in the bay the island waits, green woods
holding on, from this distance, as casually as my son
standing against the chain rail, looking at the water,
looking hard, trying to figure out something about fish
or depth, not yet sure of the question: a picture
of myself thirty-five summers ago looking into a mystery

in another part of Maine. Not a real mystery,
only a cellar hole, a family outing, the woods
around North Berwick—I can still picture
myself stepping back, my father saying come on son
see where the big house used to be. No fish
swam in that hole, but it had something to do with water.

Maybe I was scared because there wasn't any water;
anything that deep ought to be covered. My son's mystery
is his own, however. He points to a school of fish
troubling the surface fifty yards out, then the woods
on Goose Point, then Cranberry Mountain: my son,
the guide. I get my camera and take his picture.

In the background Bass Harbor Light glistens, a picture
in itself. It is four miles from us across the water,
but it seems like one. How much longer, my son
asks. Twenty minutes. The passing of time is not a mystery
to him yet. How many trees are in those woods?
I tell him more than I can count: it's like fish,

nobody knows. The water ahead is named for a fish,
Mackerel Cove. He asks if he can take a picture
of it. I agree. We pass the black gong; the woods
on shore become single trees. The tidewater
is tugging the lobster buoys and their floats—mystery
bottles hovering over the traps below. My son

asks if they had ferries when I was a son.
We watch a lobsterman pick out a large fish
from his trap and skid it along his deck, a mystery

to my son who wants to know how. I say picture
it: the bait inside the narrowing net below the water.
For the fish it's like getting lost in the woods.

As we near the shore I picture myself as my happy son,
throwing bread over the water, gulls grabbing it like fish,
mystery in his eyes, looking lovingly at the green woods.

Ballade of a rowboat

hauled from the salty grass in May
where Gleason Scott up-ended it last fall
beside his duck pen. Across the bay
a southwest breeze blew up a squall
before he got it hauled and turned: "a yawl"
he said "near Hat Island was almost blown
over and I knew she's coming all
the way." Today my son must cross alone

for the first time. It is an ordinary day
on Swan's Island: the Morrisons are checking a haul
of lobsters next door at the wharf, across the way
Russell Burns is lowering our sloop at a crawl
down his boatyard track, some seagulls brawl
over bait at a lobster boat. My son skips a stone
then dips his brush in the bottom-paint all
the way. Today my son must cross alone

because he wants to do it. I hear him say
that the harbor is not far across to our sloop, a small
speck on the shore a half-mile away;
we tip over the punt so the paint bottom falls
water side down and it steadies. He sits tall,
oars straight out. He waves once, his own
wave, and starts rowing. He will row all
the way. Today my son must cross alone.

I watch until he cannot hear my call
then drive my car the long way around. The tone
of his soft voice repeats, resounds: I can go all
the way. Today my son must cross alone.

Westward of Swan's Island

off the Hockamock Head three miles:
Sand Cove.
We dove
from our anchored sloop, freestyle-

ing over the shallow ground shells
finer than
sand, ran
the beach until our footprints fell

into the tide. The August sun
bore down.
Rolling brown
toggle buoys over the tons

of shell grains baking in the curve
of shore
we bore
down too. The hard foam swerved,

jumped hand to hand, touching each
other, island
to island.
We sailed to Marshall Island on a close reach

and played in the summer ways. We
even found
high aground
a bottle with a letter, tossed into the sea

four months before off the Tuckernuck Shoals
buoy, mapped
and capped
with wax in Nantucket Sound by souls

crossing in the spring on the underside of
Massachusetts Bay
the way
we once had crossed, with wine and the love

of the day. We hoisted sails before
the beach.
The reach
of land called Devil's Head passed by. The shore

of one island became the shore of the last:
Scrag, Ringtown
Gooseberry, John.
We ran before the wind as the sea passed.

Markings

Here in a rift of the island ledge
I watch the morning shore. Voices
from Red Point drift down, my children's
play. It is late July, the tide
is coming in. Effortlessly, a gull
rises, drops a hermit crab on a rock

and eats. White wings mark the rock
among a million stones marked off by ledge:
a seawall beach of stones, the color of gulls'
eggs, basking. I cannot sound the voices
in those stones. I count sails and tides,
I count the days. I count the ways my children

grow here by the shore before their own children
come and go. My sons bounce rocks
off bigger rocks into the sea—the tides
will bring them back more round (even the ledges
wear away). A schooner tacks, voices
carry. Three jibs luff like flailing gulls.

Last week an eagle flew by, harassed by gulls.
We were eating supper. One of the children
shouted, "The eagle!" We jumped up, our voices
marking its flight across the beach rocks,
over the spruces behind Red Point ledge—
then it was gone like a speck into the tide.

I watch the rockweed weaving in the tide.
A southwest breeze blows up, two gulls
take off. The gong off Sunken Money Ledge
sounds its iron sound, unlike my children
edging down the shore: they jump from rock
to ledge to rock, calling. Their voices

sound across the beach like porpoise voices
sounding in the blue. They stare at the tide-
line moving over the darkening rocks.

They keep track of their day: gulls,
boats, herons, seals—the way that children
do. They wave, crossing behind my ledge.

Summer children mark their island ways. The tide
marks every rock along the beach. Soon the nearby gulls
will watch from this ledge: I hear them now above my voice.

Swan's Island, August 9, 1974

A summer morning,
my son and I are running the Red Point Road
for time: for the early breeze,
the half-high sun.
                    Elsie Gillespie is picking raspberries
by her barn-garage. She waves. Overhead
the eagle from the Sisters winds slowly higher,
pacing.
        Pace will bring us home. My son
eases ahead in his long strides. There's a parked car
off the road for blueberries: summer
people. A bandana-head looks up from serious picking.

Pacing. At the turn of the woods
a crow jumps from the top of a spruce tree
caw, cawing to cronies deeper in: they
take off, protesting.
                    I relax into pace. unclench
my fists, try not to think of running.
My son disappears down the hill
through the Otter Pond swamp.
I love my son. I will catch him if I can.

Two miles—from the seawall field to Rosy Staples' house
and back. (We will sit on the deck, pick
berries by the shore, wade in the tide pool,
breathe easy.)
            Pacing. The halfway mark, my son is coming
back. We nod. Arms loose, legs
easy, I am turning
home. Pace will bring me home. I
will not think of running. The island
is cool and green, the day is long,
my son is running like the rhyme,
if you
can, if
you can, . . .
I'm running after the gingerbread man.